COUNCIL *on*
FOREIGN
RELATIONS

Rachel Vogelstein

Ending Child Marriage

How Elevating the
Status of Girls Advances
U.S. Foreign Policy Objectives

The Council on Foreign Relations (CFR) is an independent, nonpartisan membership organization, think tank, and publisher dedicated to being a resource for its members, government officials, business executives, journalists, educators and students, civic and religious leaders, and other interested citizens in order to help them better understand the world and the foreign policy choices facing the United States and other countries. Founded in 1921, CFR carries out its mission by maintaining a diverse membership, with special programs to promote interest and develop expertise in the next generation of foreign policy leaders; convening meetings at its headquarters in New York and in Washington, DC, and other cities where senior government officials, members of Congress, global leaders, and prominent thinkers come together with CFR members to discuss and debate major international issues; supporting a Studies Program that fosters independent research, enabling CFR scholars to produce articles, reports, and books and hold roundtables that analyze foreign policy issues and make concrete policy recommendations; publishing *Foreign Affairs*, the preeminent journal on international affairs and U.S. foreign policy; sponsoring Independent Task Forces that produce reports with both findings and policy prescriptions on the most important foreign policy topics; and providing up-to-date information and analysis about world events and American foreign policy on its website, CFR.org.

The Council on Foreign Relations takes no institutional positions on policy issues and has no affiliation with the U.S. government. All views expressed in its publications and on its website are the sole responsibility of the author or authors.

For further information about CFR or this paper, please write to the Council on Foreign Relations, 58 East 68th Street, New York, NY 10065, or call Communications at 212.434.9888. Visit CFR's website, www.cfr.org.

Contents

Acknowledgments vii

Introduction 1

Understanding Child Marriage 3

Implications for U.S. Foreign Policy 13

Policy Considerations 23

Conclusion 31

Endnotes 33
About the Author 41

Acknowledgments

This report is the product of several consultations with CFR's child marriage advisory group, a distinguished group of experts in international development, women's and girls' empowerment, public health, education, economic growth, and the domestic and international policy communities. Over the past six months, members of this advisory group have participated in meetings, reviewed drafts, and shared research and insights from their work on child marriage. The report has been enhanced considerably by the expertise of this advisory group; a list of the members can be found at www.cfr.org/child_marriage_report. The views expressed herein and any errors are my own.

A special acknowledgment is extended to James M. Lindsay, CFR's director of studies, and Isobel Coleman, director of CFR's Women and Foreign Policy program, for their support for this project. I am grateful to Gayle Lemmon, Anya Schmemann, Patricia Dorff, Ashley Bregman, and Charles Landow for their review of previous drafts and to Seth Goldstein, Ashley Harden, Ella Lipin, and Rebecca Stellato for their excellent assistance in the production of this paper. This report was published under the auspices of the Women and Foreign Policy program and was made possible in part by generous support from Lou Anne Jensen, Janet McKinley, and Sandy Meyer.

Rachel Vogelstein
May 2013

Introduction

The practice of child marriage is a violation of human rights. Every day, girls around the world are forced to leave their families, marry against their will, endure sexual and physical abuse, and bear children while still in childhood themselves. This practice is driven by poverty, deeply embedded cultural traditions, and pervasive discrimination against girls. According to some human rights experts, it is tantamount to sexual slavery. Yet in many parts of the world, this ancient practice still flourishes: estimates show that nearly five million girls are married under the age of fifteen every year, and some are as young as eight or nine years old.[1]

Child marriage, however, is not simply a human rights violation. It is also a threat to the prosperity and stability of the countries in which it is prevalent and undermines U.S. development and foreign policy priorities. Child marriage perpetuates poverty over generations and is linked to poor health, curtailed education, violence, instability, and disregard for the rule of law. Its effects are harmful not only to girls, but also to families, communities, and economies—and to U.S. interests—around the globe.

Given the worldwide prevalence of child marriage and its relationship to U.S. foreign policy priorities, it merits a higher place on the international agenda. In recent years, the U.S. government has enacted a comprehensive policy framework that recognizes the promotion of gender equality as a cornerstone of U.S. foreign policy.[2] Congress has underscored this strategic focus on gender equality by passing a law that mandates the secretary of state to develop a strategy to combat child marriage.[3] To meet this new requirement, the United States should raise child marriage more prominently in its diplomatic relations with affected states; increase funding to combat this practice; target its investments; and improve research, monitoring, and evaluation in this area. American leadership on child marriage will simultaneously raise the status of girls and advance critical U.S. foreign policy objectives around the world.

Understanding Child Marriage

PREVALENCE

Child marriage—also referred to as early and forced marriage—is a practice that has persisted for centuries. Today, it is defined as a formal or customary union in which one or both parties are under the age of eighteen.[4] This practice takes place across regions, cultures, and religions, and though it plagues children of both sexes, girls are disproportionately affected.

The global prevalence of child marriage is on a downward trajectory, particularly among younger girls; however, progress in curbing this tradition has been slow, and in some places the problem remains intractable.[5] The sheer number of women married as children is staggering: the United Nations estimates that in 2011 one in three women aged twenty to twenty-four—almost seventy million—had married under the age of eighteen.[6] Many of these women were far younger than eighteen at the time of their marriage; in fact, more than twenty-three million were married or in a union before the age of fifteen, which amounts to about thirteen thousand girls under fifteen being married every day. Given current trends, experts predict that by 2020, some fifty million girls will be married before they reach their fifteenth birthdays.[7]

The practice of child marriage is found in every region of the globe and is entrenched in many parts of the developing world (see Figures 1, 2, and 3). South Asia is home to the largest number of married girls: almost half of women aged twenty to twenty-four (46 percent) were married before the age of eighteen, and nearly one-fifth (18 percent) were married by age fifteen. India has the largest number of married girls in the world, accounting for 40 percent of all child marriages worldwide. Bangladesh has the highest prevalence of child marriage in South Asia, with 66 percent of young women married before age eighteen and 32 percent married before age fifteen.[8]

FIGURE 1: CHILD MARRIAGE PREVALENCE BY REGION (MARRIED BY AGE EIGHTEEN)

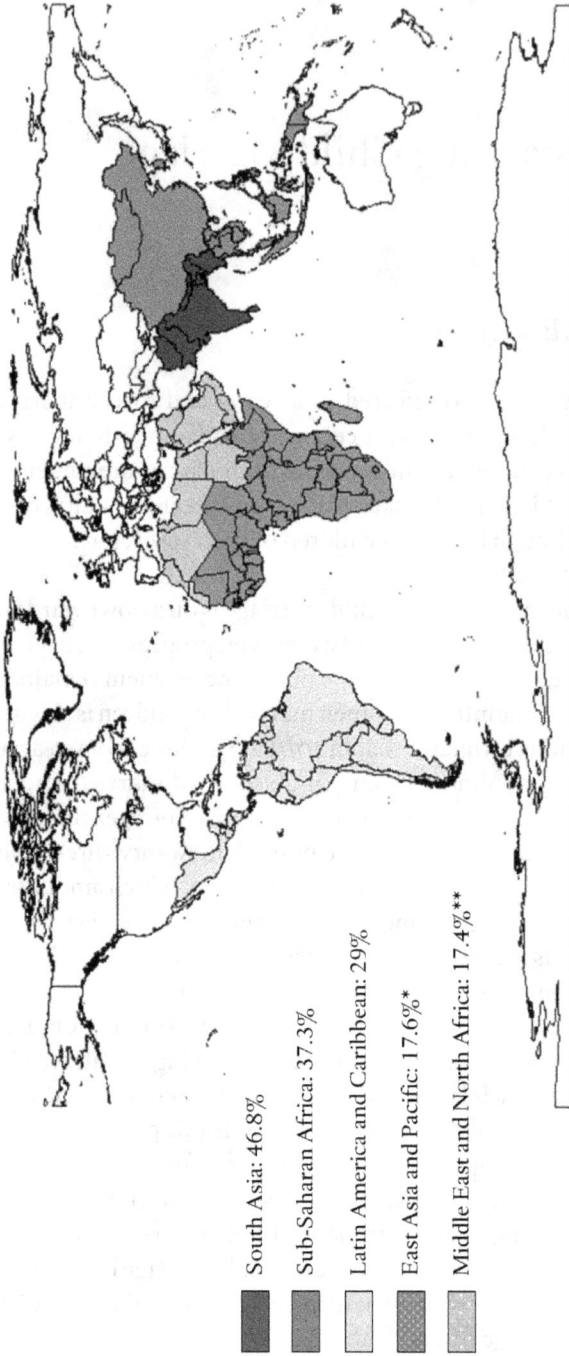

South Asia: 46.8%

Sub-Saharan Africa: 37.3%

Latin America and Caribbean: 29%

East Asia and Pacific: 17.6%*

Middle East and North Africa: 17.4%**

*Excludes China due to lack of available data.

**Excludes Bahrain, Iran, Israel, Kuwait, Libya, Oman, Qatar, Saudi Arabia, Tunisia, and the United Arab Emirates due to lack of available data.

Source: Statistics and Monitoring Section, Division of Policy and Strategy, UNICEF (2013).

FIGURE 2: COUNTRIES WITH HIGHEST PREVALENCE OF CHILD MARRIAGE

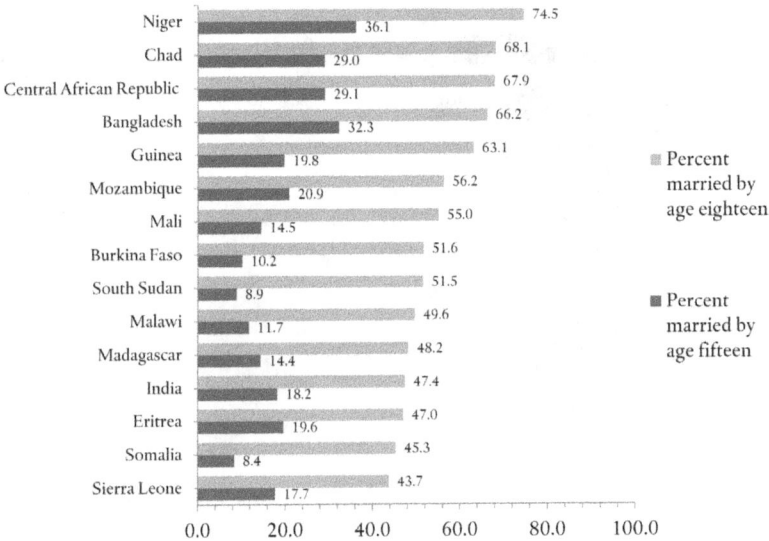

Country	Percent married by age fifteen	Percent married by age eighteen
Niger	36.1	74.5
Chad	29.0	68.1
Central African Republic	29.1	67.9
Bangladesh	32.3	66.2
Guinea	19.8	63.1
Mozambique	20.9	56.2
Mali	14.5	55.0
Burkina Faso	10.2	51.6
South Sudan	8.9	51.5
Malawi	11.7	49.6
Madagascar	14.4	48.2
India	18.2	47.4
Eritrea	19.6	47.0
Somalia	8.4	45.3
Sierra Leone	17.7	43.7

Notes: Calculations based on population of women twenty to twenty-four years old (2011). Excludes China, Bahrain, Iran, Israel, Kuwait, Libya, Oman, Qatar, Saudi Arabia, Tunisia, and the United Arab Emirates, among other countries, due to lack of available data.

Source: Statistics and Monitoring Section, Division of Policy and Strategy, UNICEF (2013).

Sub-Saharan Africa also bears a significant portion of the child marriage epidemic, with almost 40 percent of women aged twenty to twenty-four married before age eighteen and 12 percent married before age fifteen. This practice is particularly pervasive in West and Central Africa. Niger has the highest child marriage prevalence rate in the world, with approximately 75 percent of young women in a marriage or union before age eighteen and 36 percent married before age fifteen. In Chad, the Central African Republic, Guinea, Mozambique, and Eritrea, between 20 and 30 percent of women aged twenty to twenty-four were married or in a union before they turned fifteen.[9]

In Latin America and the Caribbean, 29 percent of women aged twenty to twenty-four were married by age eighteen and 7 percent were married by age fifteen. In Brazil, almost three million women aged twenty to twenty-four were married by age eighteen in 2011.

FIGURE 3: TOTAL NUMBER OF WOMEN AGED TWENTY TO
TWENTY-FOUR MARRIED OR IN A UNION BEFORE AGE
FIFTEEN (IN THOUSANDS)

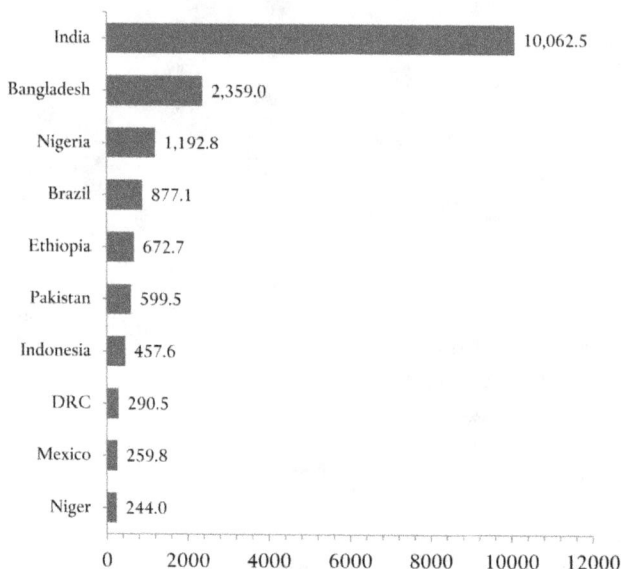

India	10,062.5
Bangladesh	2,359.0
Nigeria	1,192.8
Brazil	877.1
Ethiopia	672.7
Pakistan	599.5
Indonesia	457.6
DRC	290.5
Mexico	259.8
Niger	244.0

Notes: Calculations based on population of women twenty to twenty-four years old (2011). Excludes China, Bahrain, Iran, Israel, Kuwait, Libya, Oman, Qatar, Saudi Arabia, Tunisia, and the United Arab Emirates, among other countries, due to lack of available data.

Source: Statistics and Monitoring Section, Division of Policy and Strategy, UNICEF (2013).

Guatemala, Haiti, the Dominican Republic, and Nicaragua all have child marriage prevalence rates of 30 percent or greater.[10]

In the Middle East and North Africa, 17 percent of women aged twenty to twenty-four are married by age eighteen.[11] However, this relatively low estimate is likely skewed due to a lack of reliable data. Official figures are unavailable in more than half of the countries in the region, including Bahrain, Iran, Libya, Oman, Qatar, the United Arab Emirates, and Saudi Arabia—a country that has no minimum age of marriage.

Although child marriage is uncommon in Western democracies such as the United States, the United Kingdom, Canada, and Australia, recent studies suggest that immigrant and diaspora populations in these countries are perpetuating the practice. In 2011, the British government handled approximately fifteen hundred forced marriage cases, half of which involved girls under the age of eighteen, and a majority of which involved immigrants from Pakistan, Bangladesh, and India. A 2011 survey by the U.S.-based Tahirih Justice Center, an organization that serves immigrant women, uncovered as many as three thousand instances of known or suspected forced marriages in the United States, many involving girls under the age of eighteen.[12]

CAUSES

The origins of child marriage are multidimensional and deeply rooted. Historically, early marriage was used as a tool to maximize fertility in the context of high mortality rates. Child marriage was also employed to further economic, political, or social relationships.[13] Today, this tradition is motivated by poverty and social and cultural norms and is perpetuated by the low status of girls and women.

Economic considerations are fundamental to the practice of child marriage. In impoverished and rural areas, where this tradition is most prevalent, limited educational and economic opportunities for girls increase their dependency on male breadwinners. This reality is underscored by global data showing that women and girls with greater means marry later.[14] Moreover, economic transactions related to marriage often place a value on youth, which drives poor families to marry off their daughters to increase their own economic stability. Traditions such as dowry—in which the bride's family provides money, goods, or property to the groom—can be less expensive when paid on behalf of young brides, creating an economic incentive for early marriage. Practices such as bride price or bride wealth—in which the groom's family gives money or property to the bride's—also encourage early marriage under the theory that younger brides have a higher value because they can contribute more over time to the groom and his family.[15] Ending abusive marriages can be especially difficult if a bride's family is not able to repay money or goods received at the time of marriage, which can leave girls trapped and exposed to violence.

Regional or national instability, including conflict, displacement, and natural disaster, are also associated with the practice of child marriage. Recent research suggests that families in crisis situations are more likely to marry their daughters early, either to preserve resources by offloading economic responsibility for their girl children or in an attempt to ensure their daughters' safety from conflict-related sexual violence.[16]

By any definition, Yemen is a fragile state. In the wake of the Arab Spring, Yemen is grappling with weak governance, civil conflict, and terrorism. It also faces economic challenges: it is the poorest nation in the Arab world and has shortages of even basic services like electricity and water.[17] Approximately one in ten children does not survive past his or her fifth birthday.[18] In this context, Yemen's rate of child marriage—a practice that exacerbates many of the development challenges it faces, including maternal and child mortality, illiteracy, and economic deprivation—may contribute to even greater instability.

From her best-selling book, many have heard the story of the Yemeni girl Nujood Ali, perhaps the world's youngest divorcée. Married at the age of ten to a man three times her age, Ali was forced to drop out of school and subjected to violence and sexual abuse. Despite her young age, she summoned the courage to take herself to the courthouse and demand a divorce.[19] Her action brought international attention to the practice of child marriage in Yemen, which has the highest known prevalence in the Middle East and North Africa (MENA) region: 32 percent of Yemeni girls are married before age eighteen and 11 percent before age fifteen. In urban areas girls may be married by age twelve or thirteen, and in rural areas by age eight. In one survey, more than half of the women and girls interviewed indicated that they had no voice in choosing their spouse.[20]

Poverty and sociocultural factors in Yemen fuel this practice, but the absence of legal protections is also significant. Yemen is one of only four countries in the world without a law governing the minimum age of marriage, despite its status as a party to international treaties establishing eighteen as the minimum age. In 1999, Yemen repealed its law establishing the minimum age of marriage, which previously had set the minimum age at fifteen, due to Islamist pressures. In 2009, a proposal to set the minimum age at seventeen was defeated by parliamentarians who considered it "un-Islamic."[21] Although Yemen does have laws mandating birth and marriage registrations, these provisions are largely unenforced, which contributes to the proliferation of child marriage.[22] And the effects of this practice are profound: women and girls who were married before age twenty account for 74 percent of all maternal deaths in Yemen, which has one of the highest rates in the MENA region.[23]

Despite these challenges, some promising programs to combat the harms of child marriage have emerged. In 2005, with funds from Danida, the Danish development agency, Oxfam spearheaded the Integrated Action on Poverty and Early Marriage (IAPE) program, a three-year pilot project to reduce child marriage by raising community awareness and providing micro-leases and business development services to women in communities affected by this practice. Oxfam's evaluation found that the program fostered understanding of the negative ramifications of child marriage and delayed marriage for some girls, typically to age eighteen. The program also improved women's income levels and employment opportunities, as well as community attitudes toward women's employment.[24]

In addition, in 2009, the U.S. Agency for International Development (USAID) supported a pilot program, called Safe Age of Marriage, to change community attitudes and provide health services in the al-Sawd and al-Doodah districts. The program, led by the nongovernmental organization (NGO) Pathfinder, reached nearly twenty-nine thousand people. To ensure community legitimacy, it targeted religious leaders as champions of the program. Members from one community were even inspired to build a girls' school with a female principal. Outgoing surveys showed across-the-board increases in understanding of the benefits of delayed marriage.[25]

These programs notwithstanding, Nujood Ali's story illustrates the difficulty of shifting the norms and conditions that permit child marriage to flourish in Yemen. The proceeds of her book about her experience as a child bride were supposed to fund her education, but recent news reports indicate that, instead, Ali's father spent the money to marry additional wives and has arranged for her younger sister to marry a man twice her age.[26]

In addition, social and cultural norms create pressure to marry girls at young ages. Some parents support early marriage to protect young girls from sexual violence. Others promote it as a way to avoid premarital intimacy and pregnancy in places where loss of virginity or out-of-wedlock births would bring shame or dishonor.[27] Some communities subscribe to cultural beliefs that marrying young girls will protect or bring blessings on families.[28]

At the root of child marriage is the poor status of girls and women. The low value ascribed to girls renders them particularly susceptible to economic and cultural pressures. Endemic son preference and restrictive notions about the appropriate role for women limit investments in female education, skills, and economic potential, which further reinforces perceptions of girls as drains on family resources.

LEGAL FRAMEWORK

Several international agreements—including the Universal Declaration of Human Rights; the Convention on Consent to Marriage, Minimum Age for Marriage, and Registration of Marriages; and the Convention on the Elimination of All Forms of Discrimination against Women—limit marriage or unions to parties over the age of eighteen and emphasize that consent is an essential component of marriage.[29] Although the international standard is clear, national laws governing the legal age of marriage vary considerably.

The majority of countries around the world has set the minimum age of marriage at eighteen. However, most of these laws, including those in the United States, allow exceptions if parental or judicial consent is obtained. Some countries, such as Botswana, Mali, and Zimbabwe, make exceptions for the minimum age of marriage under customary or religious law.[30] Many countries also set lower minimum ages of marriage for girls than for boys: for example, in Iran, boys are permitted to marry at fifteen, and girls at thirteen; in Indonesia, boys are permitted at nineteen, and girls at sixteen; and in Bahrain, boys are permitted at eighteen, and girls at fifteen.[31] Four countries—Yemen, Saudi Arabia, Gambia, and Equatorial Guinea—have no enforceable law establishing the minimum age of marriage (see Figure 4).[32]

Data collection on minimum age of marriage laws is inconsistent and often outdated, and little information exists on how frequently consent or other exceptions are employed. In places where child marriage is common, parental or judicial prerogatives—whether economic or cultural—are frequently at odds with the preferences and best interests of children. The high rates of child marriage around the world, including in places with laws establishing the minimum legal age of marriage, suggest that parental consent and other exceptions can undermine the efficacy of legal protections. Even where laws are strong, lax enforcement is often a problem, and in some communities where child marriage is prevalent, implementation of child marriage laws is violently resisted.[33] In this context, it is unsurprising that the relationship between child marriage laws and prevalence rates is not predictive: some countries—such as Bangladesh and Sierra Leone—have strong laws but high prevalence rates, while other countries—such as Lebanon—have low prevalence rates, notwithstanding weak laws with exceptions that permit early marriages.[34]

Despite these challenges, minimum age of marriage laws are a powerful condemnation by the state of the practice of child marriage and passage of such laws can serve as a critical tool for advocates. In some places, legal enforcement has been effective: Macedonia has incorporated forced marriage, which is defined to include child marriage, under its definition of trafficking and prosecutes accordingly.[35] The UK has

FIGURE 4: COUNTRIES WITHOUT MINIMUM AGE OF MARRIAGE LAWS

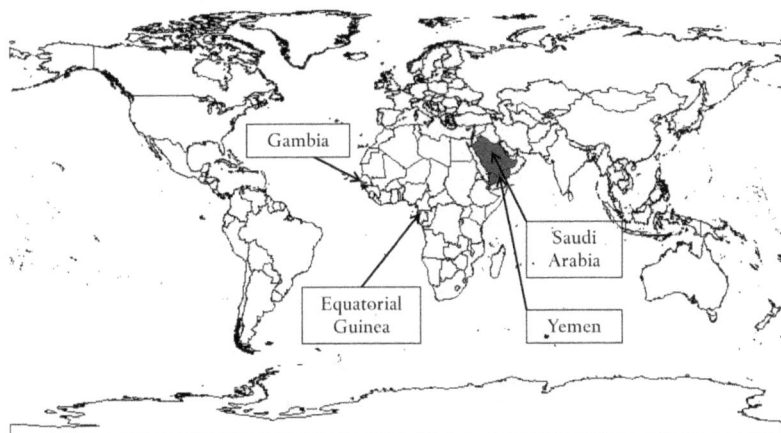

Sources: UN Statistics Division (2012) and Equality Now (2012).

created a Forced Marriage Protection Unit and enacted a law to provide "forced marriage protection orders"—similar to restraining orders—to help keep victims safe.[36] The Australian parliament recently passed an antislavery law criminalizing the practice of forced marriage, which will grant police greater investigative powers.[37]

Other laws that enshrine the secondary status of women and girls contribute to the environment in which child marriage often flourishes. Legal dowry or bride price practices foster the bartering of young girls, as do customary laws that sanction the marriage of girls to settle debts or feuds. Marital rape exemptions, including laws that pardon rapists who subsequently marry their victims, legalize sexual violence against girls in the context of marriage. Discriminatory property, inheritance, and divorce laws diminish the economic prospects and bargaining power of girls, as do discriminatory nationality laws that can leave girls unable to access public education or employment.[38] The failure of some governments to implement systems of birth and marriage registration also makes it easier to avoid compliance with minimum age of marriage laws.

Implications for U.S. Foreign Policy

The practice of child marriage has long been considered a violation of human rights. The moral case against this practice—which robs young girls of their education and economic potential, exposes them to sexual violence and abuse, increases their likelihood of early childbearing and contraction of HIV, and prematurely ends their childhood—is powerful. However, in addition to the human rights implications of early and forced marriage, this tradition traps girls and their children in a cycle of poor health, illiteracy, poverty, and violence that has consequences for development, prosperity, and stability. As such, child marriage undermines U.S. aid investments and foreign policy objectives around the world.

HEALTH

Child marriage has serious ramifications for several U.S. development priorities. Consider, for example, global health: the U.S. Global Health Initiative (GHI) promotes gender equality and the empowerment of women and girls as a primary objective because of the strong connection between the status of women and the health, education, and well-being of families and communities.[39] Under GHI, the United States has elevated investments in maternal and child health, family planning, and child nutrition. However, these efforts are jeopardized by the practice of child marriage.

Early marriage and childbearing are correlated with poor maternal health. Child brides are frequently unable to negotiate sexual relationships with their husbands and lack access to contraception, which leads to early childbearing; of the sixteen million adolescent girls who give birth every year, approximately 90 percent are married.[40] Pregnancy in adolescence truncates physical growth and increases the risk of

COUNTRY PROFILE: ETHIOPIA

In some respects, Ethiopia is an emerging success story, as it has experienced a sharp decline in rates of child marriage in recent years, most notably in Tigray, in the north, and in Gambella, in the west. Despite this progress, other regions are plagued with persistently high rates of child marriage, and Ethiopia's national prevalence rate of 41 percent remains one of the highest in the world.[41] Ethiopia's geographically varied experience with child marriage exemplifies the importance of addressing this issue at the subnational level.

In the Amhara region, for example, the problem of child marriage is widespread: 52 percent of girls there are married before the age of fifteen and 25 percent give birth before age eighteen.[42] A survey by the Population Council found that 85 percent of girls in Amhara did not have any warning they were going to be married, 95 percent did not know their husbands before marriage, 81 percent said their first sexual experience was physically forced, and over 66 percent had not reached puberty by that encounter.[43] More than half of the child brides in Amhara are married to a man at least ten years older.[44]

The Ethiopian government has taken steps to reduce child marriage. In 1997, the government developed a national action plan to address harmful traditional practices, including child marriage; the Ministry of Women, Children, and Youth Affairs is currently updating this strategy in preparation for a national workshop on child marriage to be held later this year. In addition, in 2001, a revision to Ethiopia's family code raised the minimum legal age of marriage from fifteen to eighteen. However, enforcement remains a challenge: in the Oromia region, forced child marriages through abduction stopped after a judge sentenced one abductor to eight years in prison, but resumed after the perpetrator was freed by an appellate court.[45]

One program that has achieved success in delaying marriage is Berhane Hewan—Amharic for Light for Eve—a pilot program in Mosebo, Amhara, implemented by the Ethiopian government and funded by the United Nations, the UN Foundation, and the Nike Foundation, with technical assistance from the Population

COUNTRY PROFILE: ETHIOPIA continued

Council. Berhane Hewan aimed to reduce child marriage by providing school supplies to girls to keep them in school and offering
economic incentives—in this case, a goat—to families who agreed
to delay marriage for their daughters and keep them in school for
two years.[46] During this program, girls aged ten to fourteen were
three times more likely to be in school and young girls were 90
percent less likely to be married. In the year in which the program
launched, no girls under fifteen were married.[47] The Department
for International Development (DFID), the British development
agency, and USAID are supporting efforts by the Ethiopian government to evaluate, replicate, and scale up this program.[48]

complications, and early motherhood is a significant cause of maternal mortality and morbidity: girls aged fifteen to nineteen are twice as
likely to die from causes related to pregnancy or childbirth than women
in their twenties, and girls under the age of fifteen are five times more
likely to die. Complications from pregnancy and childbirth are the
leading cause of death for girls aged fifteen to nineteen in the developing world.[49] Prolonged or obstructed labor is common for adolescent
mothers and can lead to debilitating conditions, such as obstetric fis-
tula, a hole in the birth canal that causes incontinence and results in
shame and social ostracization.

The effects of early marriage and childbearing on child health are
equally significant: stillbirths and infant mortality are 50 percent more
likely when mothers are under the age of twenty, and the risks of prema-
turity, low birth weight, and childhood malnutrition increase as well.[50]
Evidence also shows that when mothers die in childbirth, their children
are also more likely to suffer: children whose mothers die are up to ten
times more likely to die themselves within two years.[51] Even when adolescent mothers do survive, their children face a higher risk of poor
health because married girls tend to have more children and shorter
birth spacing than married adult women. This, in turn, increases the
probability of adverse health outcomes and can tax family resources,
perpetuating generations of poverty and deprivation.[52]

Child marriage also puts girls at greater risk of sexually transmitted infections, including HIV. Married girls are more likely than unmarried adolescents or married adult women to have unprotected sexual relations, in part because of limited authority in marriages that are frequently characterized by significant age differences.[53] A study of twenty-nine countries in Africa and Latin America revealed that girls who marry at young ages tend, on average, to have husbands who are five to fourteen years older, which can create an insurmountable power differential and preclude autonomous decision-making.[54] Husbands of married girls are not only older but also more likely to be HIV-positive than partners of unmarried girls, and in polygamous societies, a child bride may be one of several wives, further increasing her possible exposure to HIV.[55] Married girls also may not have access to information about HIV or how to protect against transmission. The transmission of HIV has ramifications not only on the health of married girls, but on their children and families, as child brides who contract HIV can transmit the virus to their children during pregnancy, may be unable to provide long-term care for their relatives, and may infect future partners.

Delaying marriage and childbirth can prevent many of these poor outcomes and pay dividends for the health of mothers and their children and the development of entire communities and economies. Postponing marriage can reduce the risk of contracting HIV and other sexually transmitted infections. Deferring childbirth until after the age of eighteen reduces the risk of maternal mortality and morbidity. Delaying pregnancy also has positive effects on the health and education of children: mortality is less likely and good nutrition is more likely, which can lead to better cognition, education, and economic outcomes.[56]

EDUCATION

The education of girls, long considered one of the single most effective development investments that can be made, is another top U.S. aid priority shortchanged by child marriage.[57] Research shows that the practice of child marriage often curtails education for young girls. One study of girls in Kenya concluded that finding a marriage partner is associated with a 78 percent increased risk of termination of secondary schooling.[58] Other studies demonstrate that early marriage in parts of sub-Saharan Africa and South Asia reduces the likelihood of literacy.[59]

The effects of truncated education are profound: limited schooling for girls not only undercuts their potential but can undermine economic progress. Even one extra year of schooling beyond the average can increase women's wages by 10 to 20 percent, and a World Bank study suggests that a one-percentage-point increase in the share of women with secondary education increases a country's annual per capita income growth by 0.3 percent.[60] Child survival and immunization rates are also higher for the offspring of educated mothers.[61] These benefits vanish when a girl's education is abbreviated by marriage.

Although more analysis is needed, some experts propose that limited education is not only an effect but also a cause of early marriage. Recent research indicates that education is the most critical factor in efforts to increase age at marriage; in Turkey, for instance, the extension of compulsory school to age fourteen reduced the proportion of girls married at age sixteen by 45 percent.[62] This suggests that the economic potential offered by girls' education may elevate the value of girls and reduce familial pressures to marry off their young daughters. It also suggests that the economic returns on delaying the age of marriage, which is correlated with secondary schooling for girls, may be significant not only for individual families, but also for the development of entire economies.

ECONOMIC DEVELOPMENT

The extent to which child marriage inhibits women's economic participation may subvert economic development and growth. Particularly where gender norms discourage women's economic participation, child marriage often not only ends a girl's education, thereby limiting her economic potential, but also precludes her from participating in the marketplace for years.[63] This dependence can fuel a cycle of poverty that is especially devastating to girls and their families should anything happen to their source of income; it can also undermine the growth potential of entire communities.[64] Women are drivers of economic growth—in particular, through small and medium enterprises—in many parts of the world.[65] Inclusion of women in the workforce has been shown to increase overall GDP, and narrowing gender gaps in certain economies could dramatically increase per capita incomes.[66] Women are also more likely to spend their income on food and health care for their children, which has positive implications for economic growth.[67] This economic potential is lost in places where child marriage effectively removes girls from the public sphere.

Evidence also suggests that the practice of child marriage is less stable than marriage between adults and puts young girls—and their children—on a trajectory of poverty and disadvantage. Although child marriage is often promoted to prevent out-of-wedlock birth and single motherhood, young girls are more likely to become single mothers through divorce or widowhood than through premarital birth, in part because of the age gap between child brides and their husbands.[68] Child marriage, then, often begets single mothers who are hampered by limited resources, which in turn traps their children in a cycle of poverty and increases the likelihood of child mortality.[69]

STABILITY

U.S. interests in stability and security are also undermined by the practice of child marriage. This tradition is highly correlated with domestic and sexual violence, which is destabilizing not only to girls but also to others in their households and communities. Data from India show that girls married at age eighteen or older are more likely to repudiate domestic violence, whereas those married under the age of eighteen are more likely to have experienced either physical or sexual abuse.[70] Girls married as children are also more likely to be physically abused not only by their husbands, but also by their family members and in-laws. Wide disparities in age and power between husband and wife, as well as marital financial transactions such as dowry and bride price, can exacerbate social norms that sanction violence. Some scholars propose that sexual and physical abuse have ramifications far outside of the walls of a home; recent research suggests that violence against girls and women is correlated with civil strife and conflict.[71]

U.S. commitments to promoting stability through adherence to the rule of law are also undermined by the prevalence of child marriage. International and national laws governing the minimum age of marriage and the protection of children and prohibiting violence and sexual abuse are routinely violated around the world. In some places, attempted enforcement of these laws is met with indifference; in others, with violent resistance—for example, in rural parts of India, where government

COUNTRY PROFILE: INDIA

India is a fast-developing nation, but experts predict the many obstacles preventing women from participating fully in India's economy will undermine the country's continued development.[72] This is particularly true with respect to the problem of child marriage, which curtails the education and economic prospects of significant portions of the population.

Almost half of Indian girls are married before age eighteen, and given its massive population, the country accounts for some 40 percent of the world's known child brides—more than ten million.[73] In several states, including Andhra Pradesh, Jharkhand, and Rajasthan, 20 percent of girls are married before the age of fifteen.[74] Child marriages are still celebrated en masse, in public festivals sometimes involving children under ten, or even toddlers, who effectively are betrothed until puberty.[75] Those married as girls report twice as many instances of beatings and threats by their husbands, and three times as many instances of rape, as women married as adults.[76] Although the prevalence of child marriage for girls under fifteen has dropped by nearly one-third, from 26.1 percent in 1993 to 18 percent in 2011, considerable work remains.[77]

Prosecutions to enforce India's minimum age of marriage, set since 1978 at eighteen for girls and twenty-one for boys, have traditionally been rare.[78] However, in recent years, the Indian government has taken measures to reduce child marriage. In 2000, to help enforce the law on the minimum age of marriage, the government required all married couples to register their ages and provide consent prior to marrying. In Uttar Pradesh, the government initiated an awareness campaign around the legal age of marriage and denied eligibility for government jobs to those who married underage after the policy took effect.[79] In 2006, India passed the Prohibition of Child Marriage Act, which increased the penalties for conducting a child marriage ceremony, made a child marriage voidable by a married party up to two years after reaching the age of maturity, and provided for court intervention in the form of stay orders.[80] However, despite these improvements, legal inconsistencies undermine the effectiveness of these statutes. For example, some Indian laws continue to establish the age of majority at fourteen and statutory rape within a marriage is recognized only if a girl is under fifteen.[81]

In addition to legal reform, state governments in India have established programs to help curtail child marriage. One such program, initiated by the Haryana state government in 1994, provides conditional cash transfers to families and girls who delay marriage until age eighteen. Called Apni Beti, Apna Dhan—Hindi for Our Daughter, Our Wealth—the program provides a mother who gives birth to a girl with eleven dollars to partially compensate for childbirth costs. The program also capitalizes a savings account for the newborn girl worth $54, to which the girl is entitled at age eighteen—at an expected value of $540 or more—provided that she remains unmarried.[82] This account is meant to counteract the incentive for families to obtain a bride price through a daughter's marriage and may also be used to offset future dowry costs, which often rise with the bride's age. The first cohort of girls to be affected by this program began turning eighteen in 2012; the International Center for Research on Women plans to release an evaluation of the program in 2013.[83]

workers have been attacked for trying to stop the marriage of children.[84] An absence of systems of birth and marriage registration and other basic human rights protections contributes to violation of laws establishing the minimum legal age of marriage. This impunity is corrosive not only to the well-being of individual girls, but also to overall fidelity to the rule of law.

Finally, recent research suggests that the practice of child marriage is associated with instability and state fragility. One analysis shows that most of the twenty-five countries with the highest prevalence of child marriage are also either fragile states or at high risk of natural disaster.[85] Girls living through conflict and humanitarian crises are uniquely susceptible to child marriage, given that family structures, social networks, and institutions may be upended; recent research confirms that some families pursue child marriage as a social protection or poverty reduction mechanism in crisis situations—for example, in war-torn

FIGURE 5: FY 2012 U.S. FOREIGN ASSISTANCE PERTINENT TO CHILD MARRIAGE

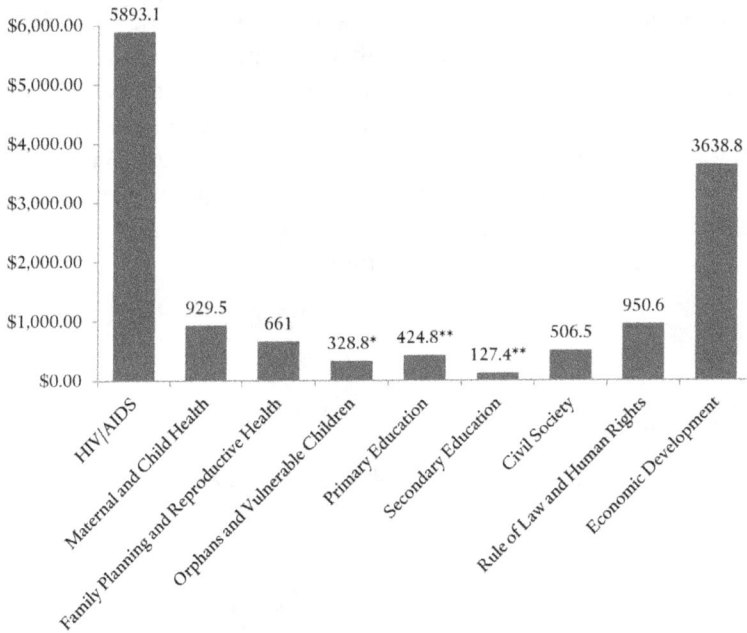

*The U.S. President's Emergency Plan for AIDS Relief (PEPFAR) FY11 Operation Plan data. FY12 data unavailable.
**Data based on percentage allocation provided by USAID.

Sources: The U.S. President's Emergency Plan for AIDS Relief (PEPFAR) FY11 Operation Plan; Foreign Assistance.gov.

states such as Syria and South Sudan, or drought-stricken countries like Niger.[86] Perpetuation of this practice in weak states, however, only exacerbates long-term poverty, illiteracy, and poor health outcomes in places already overwhelmed by numerous and complex challenges.

THE CASE AGAINST CHILD MARRIAGE

The evidence establishing a link between child marriage and ill health, illiteracy, poverty, violence, and instability cannot be ignored. U.S. foreign policy interests in stability and prosperity and U.S. investments in a range of areas—including global health, education, economic growth, and governance—are compromised wherever child marriage endures. The United States spends billions of dollars to reduce maternal and child mortality, prevent the transmission of HIV, improve educational attainment, stimulate economic growth, and promote the rule of law (see Figure 5), and has vital interests in the stability of many countries where child marriage is pervasive. Given the abundance of evidence demonstrating the devastating effect of child marriage on a range of development and security priorities, the U.S. government should address this practice to maximize returns on its aid investments and promote stability in crucial parts of the world.

Policy Considerations

CURRENT POLICY

In recent years, child marriage has received increased attention as leaders have begun to recognize how it undermines a range of development
and security priorities. The United States, which historically addressed
child marriage through small-scale development efforts, recently
strengthened policies aimed at addressing this practice. In 2012, the
Department of State required reporting on child marriage in its annual
country reports on human rights practices and instituted new guidance
and training for consular staff in U.S. embassies to strengthen assistance for U.S. citizens forced into child marriage abroad.[87] In addition,
USAID developed a policy statement on child marriage that outlined
principles for action, including a focus on the needs of already married
girls, addressing community norms, and partnering with men.[88] The
United States also included child marriage in a government-wide strategy to prevent and respond to gender-based violence around the world.[89]

On Capitol Hill, a bipartisan group of elected officials, led by Richard Durbin (D-IL) in the Senate and Betty McCollum (D-MN) and
Aaron Schock (R-IL) in the House, championed a bill to bolster U.S.
efforts to reduce the prevalence of child marriage around the world.
On the heels of several failed attempts to pass this legislation in both
houses of the legislature—in part because of concerns about language
related to women's health—provisions strengthening the U.S. response
to child marriage were included in the Violence Against Women Act
reauthorization bill, which was signed into law in March 2013.[90] These
provisions codify the Department of State's child marriage reporting
requirement in its human rights reports and mandate that the secretary
of state develop and implement a multiyear, cross-sectoral strategy to
prevent child marriage that includes both diplomatic and programmatic initiatives.

Child marriage is also beginning to enjoy a higher profile on the international stage. In April 2012, under U.S. leadership, foreign ministers from the G8 included a condemnation of early and forced marriage in the chair's statement for the first time.[91] In October 2012, United Nations secretary-general Ban Ki-moon marked the first UN International Day of the Girl Child by calling for an end to child marriage and holding a special session on this topic, together with former UN Women executive director Michelle Bachelet and UN Population Fund executive director Babatunde Osotimehin.[92] In March 2013, the UN Commission on the Status of Women held a special session on this issue and included provisions on early and forced marriage in its conclusions.[93]

In addition, the issue of child marriage has been elevated by important civil society champions. For example, The Elders—a group of prominent world figures chaired by Archbishop Desmond Tutu and including such leaders as former Norwegian prime minister Gro Harlem Brundtland, former Irish president Mary Robinson, and former U.S. president Jimmy Carter—launched Girls Not Brides, a global partnership to end child marriage, to amplify this issue on the world stage; since its launch in September 2011, Girls Not Brides has grown to a partnership of more than 250 NGOs in more than forty-five countries working on grassroots, national, and global levels.[94] Former British prime minister and current UN special envoy on education Gordon Brown, together with Sarah Brown, has taken leadership on the critical issue of combatting child marriage by promoting girls' education.

MOVING FORWARD

The Obama administration has an opportunity to capitalize on the momentum created by recent commitments on child marriage and the new requirement for a strategy addressing this issue. Evidence shows that reducing the prevalence of this practice requires a multipronged approach that promotes legal reform, educational and economic opportunity, and behavior change, and includes both top-down government reforms and bottom-up grassroots programs. As the U.S. secretary of state, administrator of USAID, and other officials craft a child marriage strategy, they should take the following steps to further U.S. interests in development, prosperity, and stability by reducing child marriage.

COUNTRY PROFILE: SENEGAL

Senegal is home to several sociocultural traditions, including female-genital mutilation (FGM) and child marriage, which harm the health and rights of girls and hinder the progress of families and communities. In Senegal and other African countries, FGM and child marriage are closely linked; the former practice is frequently a prerequisite for the latter.[95] The factors motivating both of these harmful traditions—including the desire to prevent premarital sex—are complementary.[96] Because FGM is performed around puberty and girls are expected to be married shortly thereafter, communities that practice FGM are likely to have high rates of child marriage. Girls who are not married within a year of being presented to the community after undergoing FGM are thought to be undesirable or unlucky, compounding social pressure to marry early.[97] Girls who do marry are expected to have children immediately; nearly one in ten children in Senegal is born to a mother between the ages of fifteen and nineteen, with dire ramifications for maternal and childhood mortality and morbidity.[98]

The practice of child marriage in Senegal is aided by legal exceptions to the minimum age of marriage. Although the law sets the minimum age of marriage at eighteen, it is sixteen with parental consent and thirteen with a court order. No minimum age exists if the parties contract marriage under customary law.[99] Given these gaps in the law, as well as deeply rooted cultural norms, the prevalence of this practice in Senegal remains high—particularly in the south and southeast, where more than 30 percent of girls are married by age sixteen.[100]

Thanks in part to effective community empowerment and nonformal education programs, however, the age of first marriage is slowly rising. One such program, developed by the NGO Tostan, has made considerable progress in fostering community abandonment of harmful traditional practices. Since 1997, Tostan has worked with more than five thousand Senegalese communities in comprehensive community empowerment programs that address child marriage and FGM and encourage participants to conduct outreach within their social networks.[101] As recently as January 2013, 427 additional Senegalese villages made

public declarations against child marriage and FGM; in participating villages, the proportion of girls married before age fifteen
decreased by 49 percent. Tostan has expanded its model to seven
other African countries.[102]

PRIORITIZE CHILD MARRIAGE IN U.S. DIPLOMACY

The United States should include the issue of child marriage in bilat-
eral discussions with high-prevalence countries to reduce this practice
and persuade foreign officials that it diminishes prosperity and stability. With major partners such as India, U.S. officials should prioritize
the issue in broader strategic dialogues. In fragile states such as South
Sudan and Yemen, the United States should recognize child marriage
as a determinant of security outcomes and address it accordingly. The
United States should encourage efforts by governments seeking to
tackle this issue internally—for example, in Malawi—by offering funding and technical assistance. Washington should not shy away from
stressing the importance of child marriage with allies that have disturb-
ing records on this issue—for example, Saudi Arabia, which has no law
establishing a minimum age of marriage. The United States should also
forge partnerships with committed allies, such as the UK, Australia,
Canada, and the Netherlands, to expand and leverage programmatic
and diplomatic initiatives on child marriage.

Existing diplomatic tools can help address child marriage. The
release of the Department of State's human rights reports, for example,
presents an opportunity to spotlight countries with high prevalence
rates. A further step could be a separate report, modeled after the U.S.
Trafficking in Persons report, which ranks countries based on their
efforts to combat child marriage and highlights governments that are
addressing this problem, those that have taken small steps but need to
do more, and those that neglect or fail to recognize this issue.

The United States can further elevate the issue of child marriage in
multilateral forums—for example, in the G8, where members can build
upon the 2012 foreign ministers' statement, or the G20, which includes

countries with high child marriage prevalence rates. As governments, international organizations, scholars, and NGOs embark on the formulation of sustainable development goals for the post–Millennium Development Goal era, the United States should ensure a focus on the empowerment of women and girls; to that end, Washington should support the inclusion of a child marriage indicator as a quantifiable metric of the welfare of adolescent girls and the overall status of women. Also useful would be U.S. support for resolutions against the practice of child marriage in the UN General Assembly, the UN Human Rights Council, the UN Commission on the Status of Women, and other forums.

Finally, the United States should use public-private partnerships and other collaborative mechanisms to support efforts by civil society and the private sector to combat child marriage. Given the centrality of community norms and male behavior to the perpetuation of child marriage, programs that collaborate with religious leaders and with men and boys should be a particular focus. In all diplomatic efforts, U.S. officials should be aware of sensitivity to perceptions of cultural imperialism in addressing child marriage and highlight both the universality of this practice across regions and religions as well as the evidence of its deleterious effects on prosperity and stability.

INCREASE FUNDING

Given clear evidence that child marriage endangers many U.S. priorities—including global health, education, economic development, the rule of law, and human rights—the case for increased funding to combat this practice is compelling. Indeed, devoting more resources to combating child marriage could increase the returns on American investments in a time of austerity. The United States, therefore, should increase resources to support an elevated and long-term focus on child marriage as a foreign policy and development priority and a strategic imperative. In particular, policymakers should ensure that this issue is adequately integrated into budget and policy planning in affected sectors (see Figure 5).

To facilitate interagency prioritization of child marriage, administration officials should charge the gender working group recently established by presidential memorandum and chaired by the national security adviser, the U.S. ambassador-at-large for global women's issues, and the executive director of the White House Council on Women and

Girls with the task of working internally with relevant bureaus to ensure that any child marriage strategy includes a robust, crosscutting effort to increase resources.[103] Funding for programmatic initiatives with a primary purpose of reducing child marriage or supporting married girls should be tracked, quantified, and increased as necessary. Existing programs that have a secondary or tangential effect on child marriage should be reevaluated and strengthened wherever possible to include a focus on this issue.

TARGET INVESTMENTS

The U.S. government should concentrate its aid investments both functionally and geographically. Functionally, although child marriage touches a range of important areas, evidence suggests that U.S. policy should focus on three in particular: maternal and child health, because of the link between child marriage and maternal and child mortality; family planning, given the demonstrated need for health services for young married girls; and girls' secondary education, due to the relationship between education and age at marriage. The latter area especially warrants greater U.S. attention and investment since USAID currently focuses overwhelmingly on primary education, despite strong evidence of the economic and public health returns from girls' secondary education. In addition, policymakers should consider how substantial U.S. investments in areas such as HIV/AIDS and economic development could be strengthened by integrating the issue of child marriage (see Figure 5). Policymakers also should ensure that efforts address the plight of millions of already married girls and their children around the world—a priority to which USAID has already committed.

Geographically, Washington should focus on a select group of countries to demonstrate the effect of child marriage programs and contribute to the body of evidence in this area. In choosing priority countries, policymakers should consider several sets of criteria, including prevalence rates, population size, and the age of girls affected. Policymakers should focus on countries with the highest rates of child marriage and on the subnational regions of greatest need within them, to ensure that American dollars reach those pockets—rural or otherwise—in which the need is greatest. Population size also should be considered, with giants such as India rising to the top of the list. Moreover, countries with high prevalence rates for girls under fifteen, such as Niger, Bangladesh, and several countries in West Africa, should receive special attention, given that many of the ramifications of child marriage and early child-bearing are more severe for this age group.

Another set of criteria should consider a country's broader development context, including health, education, and economic growth. For example, places identified by the Population Council as having both a high number of girls at risk of child marriage and a significant unmet need for contraception among married girls and women could be good areas for investment.[104] Other related development indicators, such as low secondary education attainment and high HIV prevalence, should be considered to leverage existing U.S. investments.

Policymakers should also consider investing in countries, such as Ethiopia, that demonstrate political will to address child marriage through national action plans, enforcement of legislation, or robust programs. Strong grassroots civil society efforts related to human rights and the rule of law, among other issues, can foster an enabling environment for community education programs to succeed and social norms to change. The United States should prioritize opportunities to co-invest with recipient governments in order to establish a sustainable and long-term approach to this issue.

Two additional considerations deserve attention. The first is broader U.S. strategic interests, with emphasis on countries where conflicts or natural disasters imperil stability. These countries, which include Afghanistan, South Sudan, and Yemen, should receive significant investment, given the links between instability and child marriage. The second consideration is global resource gaps. The United States can help close such gaps by focusing on regions where child marriage receives little attention, such as Latin America and the Caribbean, and countries like Brazil, which has the third highest number of married girls in the world.

IMPROVE RESEARCH, MONITORING, AND EVALUATION

To improve efforts to address child marriage, the United States should implement better monitoring of this practice and evaluation of programs geared toward its elimination. Internally, the U.S. government should track expenditures on child marriage programs in such areas as global health, education, economic growth, the rule of law, human rights, and civil society promotion, and it should rigorously measure and evaluate these programs. In addition, the government should collect information on the prevalence of child marriage in the United States, particularly among immigrant and diaspora communities, and consider enacting policies to protect girls on U.S. soil, consistent with the example set by the UK and Australia. The Congressional Research Service or Government Accountability Office could be enlisted to evaluate the effect of child marriage prevention efforts.

Externally, the United States should champion efforts to improve international understanding of the practice and effects of child marriage on girls, their families, and overall prosperity and stability. In particular, data gaps on child marriage prevalence in certain regions—for example, in the MENA region, in Latin America, and among diaspora communities in the Western world—should be filled. Data on laws establishing the minimum age of marriage, their enforcement, and the extent to which parental consent and other exceptions are employed should be expanded; Washington should encourage UNICEF to standardize and improve data collection in this area. Institutions such as the World Health Organization should continue efforts to document the effects of child marriage on health and other areas and offer technical assistance for addressing this practice in development programs. Finally, more research is needed on the effects of education on child marriage, the long-term economic implications of this practice, and short-term indicators of progress in changing social norms.

Conclusion

The practice of child marriage is not only a violation of the human rights of girls and a grave moral challenge; it also undermines the foreign policy priorities of the United States. In this time of austerity, policymakers should recognize that addressing child marriage is not only a moral imperative—it is also a cost-effective and strategic imperative to achieve the United States' diplomatic and development goals. The reach and success of U.S. efforts to improve global health, bolster education, foster economic growth, and promote stability and the rule of law will grow stronger if this persistent practice comes to an end.

Endnotes

1. Analysis based on data provided by the Statistics and Monitoring Section, Division of Policy and Strategy, UNICEF, January 2013.
2. See, for example, *U.S. National Security Strategy*, 2010 (stating that "countries are more peaceful and prosperous when women are accorded full and equal rights and opportunity. When those rights and opportunities are denied, countries often lag behind"); *U.S. Department of State Quadrennial Diplomacy and Development Review*, 2010 (stating that "[t]he protection and empowerment of women and girls is key to the foreign policy and security of the United States"); U.S. Department of State Policy Guidance on Gender Equality, 2012 (requiring the promotion of gender equality to be integrated as a strategic objective across the work of the department); USAID Gender Equality and Female Empowerment Policy, 2012 (outlining a strategic focus on gender equality in foreign assistance).
3. Violence Against Women Reauthorization Act of 2013, PL 113-4, March 7, 2013, 127 Stat 5.
4. Several international agreements establish the definition of child marriage as a union in which one or both parties are under age eighteen and reinforce that consent is an essential component of marriage. The Convention on the Rights of the Child (1989) defines children as people who are under the age of eighteen. The Universal Declaration of Human Rights (1948) states that "men and women of full age" have the right to marry and affirms that "[m]arriage shall be entered into only with the free and full consent of the intending spouses." The Convention on Consent to Marriage, Minimum Age for Marriage, and Registration of Marriages (1962) calls on states to establish a minimum age of marriage and a system of registration. In addition, the Convention on the Elimination of All Forms of Discrimination Against Women (1979) proclaims that "the betrothal and marriage of a child shall have no legal effect" and that women have a right to choose a spouse and enter into marriage with "free and full consent." Finally, the International Conference on Population and Development (1994) affirms the importance of increasing age at marriage.
5. See, for example, Ming Cong Nguyen and Quentin Wodon, "Child Marriage and Education," *World Bank Mimeo*, 2013 (demonstrating the worldwide decrease in child marriage prevalence over time).
6. Data provided by the Statistics and Monitoring Section, Division of Policy and Strategy, UNICEF, January 2013. The standard international indicator used to determine child marriage prevalence is the proportion of young women aged twenty to twenty-four who were married or in a union before the age of eighteen. A retrospective prevalence determination is used to capture girls aged fifteen, sixteen, and seventeen who are classified as single but may eventually marry or join a union before age eighteen. See, for example, http://www.childinfo.org/marriage_methodology.html (UNICEF). UNICEF child marriage estimates exclude China and several countries in the Middle East and North Africa because of a lack of data.

7. UNFPA, "Marrying Too Young: End Child Marriage," 2012; Joint News Release, *Every Woman Every Child/Girls Not Brides/PMNCH/United Nations Foundation/UNFPA/ UNICEF/UN Women/WHO/World Vision/World YWCA, Child Marriages: 39,000 Every Day,* March 7, 2013.

8. Analysis based on data provided by the Statistics and Monitoring Section, Division of Policy and Strategy, UNICEF, January 2013.

9. Ibid.

10. Ibid.

11. Ibid.

12. Pat Strickland, "Forced Marriage." House of Commons Library, Home Affairs Section, Standard Note: SN/HA/1003, June 8, 2012; Tahirih Justice Center, "Forced Marriage in Immigrant Communities in the United States," September 2011.

13. UNICEF, "Child Marriage and the Law," 2008, p. 23; see also UNICEF, "Early Marriage: Child Spouses"; *Innocenti Digest No. 7,* March 2001, pp. 2, 6, citing UNICEF/ WCARO, 2000; "Etude sur les mariages précoces et grossesses précoces au Burkina-Faso, Cameroun, Gambie, Liberia, Niger et Tchad" (Study on early marriages and early pregnancies in Burkina Faso, Cameroon, Gambia, Liberia, and Chad).

14. World Bank, *World Development Report on Gender Equality and Development,* 2012, p. 154, figure 4.3.

15. International Center for Research on Women, "Too Young to Wed," 2003, p. 6, citing Ruth Nasimiyu, "Changing women's rights over property in western Kenya," in Thomas S. Weisner, Candice Weisner, and Philip L. Kilbride, eds., *African Families and the Crisis of Social Change* (Westport, CT: Bergin and Garvey, 1997).

16. World Vision, "Untying the Knot: Exploring Early Marriage in Fragile States," 2013.

17. United Nations Department for Social and Economic Affairs, "Assessing Development Strategies to Achieve the MDGs in the Republic of Yemen," 2011, pp. 1, 10–11.

18. The under-five mortality rate is 78.2 per one thousand live births. United Nations Department for Social and Economic Affairs, "Assessing Development Strategies to Achieve the MDGs in the Republic of Yemen," 2011, p. 15, table 2.3, based on data provided by Central Statistics Organization and MOPIC, 2010.

19. Nujood Ali with Delphine Minoui, *I Am Nujood, Age 10 and Divorced* (New York: Crown, 2010), p. 169.

20. Analysis based on data provided by the Statistics and Monitoring Section, Division of Policy and Strategy, UNICEF, January 2013, which excludes data from more than half of countries in the MENA region, including Bahrain, Iran, Libya, Oman, Qatar, UAE, and Saudi Arabia; Human Rights Watch, Yemen, "How Come You Allow Little Girls to Get Married?," 2011, pp. 20–21, citing Abdel Majid al-Shargaby, "Early Marriage in Yemen: A Baseline Study to Combat Early Marriage in Hadhrahmawt and Hudaidah Governorates," Gender Development Research and Studies Centre, Sanaa University, 2005, pp. 4, 7, and Robert F. Worth, "Tiny Voices Defy Child Marriage in Yemen," *New York Times,* June 28, 2009.

21. "Yemen's Child Bride Backlash," *Foreign Policy,* April 30, 2010.

22. Human Rights Watch, Yemen, "How Come You Allow Little Girls to Get Married?," pp. 18, 26–27, based on analysis of UNICEF MICS (2006) birth and marriage registration data.

23. Republic of Yemen, Ministry of Health and Population, "Family Health Survey," http:// www.mophp-ye.org/arabic/docs/Familyhealth_english.pdf, p. 174. The two other countries with the highest maternal mortality rates are Djibouti and Sudan. UNICEF, "Middle East and North Africa Regional Analysis Report," 2010, p. 8. For maternal mortality ratios, see UNDP, "International Human Development Indicators: Maternal Mortality

Ratio," http://hdrstats.undp.org/en/indicators/89006.html; see also UNICEF Statistics, "Yemen: At a Glance," 2010 (suggesting that the rate may be as high as .37 percent).

24. The program focused on the population of the two governorates of Hadramaut and Hudida, made approximately one thousand micro-leases to women, and affected five thousand to fifteen thousand people. ICRW, "Solutions to End Child Marriage," 2011, pp. 19, 30, 43.

25. Pathfinder, "'Safe Age of Marriage' in Yemen: Fostering Change in Social Norms," 2010, pp. 1–3.

26. Joe Sheffer, "Child bride says father kept bestseller money," *Guardian*, March 13, 2013.

27. International Center for Research on Women, "Too Young to Wed," pp. 4–6.

28. World Vision, "Before She's Ready: 15 Places Girls Marry Before 15," 2008, p. 15, based on World Vision survey data.

29. See note 4.

30. UN Statistics Division, "Legal Age for Marriage Table 3a," December 2012, citing Botswana UNPD 2011, Mali CEDAW Report (2006), Zimbabwe CEDAW Report (2012), Cambodia CEDAW Report (2006), Eritrea CEDAW Report (2006), and El Salvador UNPD (2011); Equality Now, "Minimum Age of Marriage Update," 2012, citing Botswana CEDAW State Report (2008), Mali CEDAW Concluding Observations/Comments (February 2006), Zimbabwe CEDAW Report (November 2010).

31. UN Statistics Division, "Legal Age for Marriage Table 3a," citing Iran UNPD (2011), Indonesia CEDAW Report (2007), and Bahrain UNPD (2011); Equality Now, "Minimum Age of Marriage Update," citing Iran CRC Concluding Observations (March 2005), Indonesia CEDAW Concluding Observations (August 2007), and Bahrain CRC Concluding Observations (August 2011). Although the minimum age of marriage for girls in Iran is currently thirteen, Iran's chairman of its legal affairs committee, Mohammad Ali Isfenani, recently called for lowering the minimum age of marriage to nine so as not to contradict Sharia. See Vivian Tsai, "Child Bride Practice Rising in Iran, Parliament Seeks to Lower Girl's Legal Marriage Age to 9," *International Business Times*, August 30, 2012.

32. UN Statistics Division, "Legal Age for Marriage Table 3a," citing Yemen CEDAW Report (2002), Gambia CEDAW Report (2005), Saudi Arabia UNPD (2011), and Equatorial Guinea CEDAW Report (2004); Equality Now, "Minimum Age of Marriage Update," citing Yemen CEDAW Report (March 2007), Gambia CEDAW Report (April 2003), Saudi Arabia CEDAW Concluding Observations (April 2008), and Equatorial Guinea CEDAW Report (February 2004).

33. See, for example, PBS, *Child Brides, Stolen Lives*, http://www.pbs.org/now/shows/341/transcript.html (detailing an incident where an Indian social worker was attacked violently and lost a hand due to her attempts to stop a child marriage).

34. Data provided by the Statistics and Monitoring Section, Division of Policy and Strategy, UNICEF, January 2013; UN Statistics Division, "Legal Age for Marriage Table 3a," citing Bangladesh CEDAW Report (2004), Sierra Leone CEDAW Report (2007), and Lebanon CEDAW Report (2008); Equality Now, "Minimum Age of Marriage Update," citing Bangladesh CEDAW Report (2004), Sierra Leone CEDAW Report (2011), and Lebanon CEDAW Report (2007).

35. Cheryl Thomas et al., *Developing Legislation on Violence Against Women and Girls*, UNIFEM Virtual Knowledge Centre to End Violence Against Women and Girls, 2013, pp. 364–66.

36. Ibid.

37. Crimes Legislation Amendment (Slavery, Slavery-Like Conditions and People Trafficking) Bill 2012, signed into law March 7, 2013, http://www.aph.gov.au/Parliamentary_Business/Bills_Legislation/Bills_Search_Results/Result?bId=r4840.

38. For example, in India, inheritance law reforms are associated with increases in age of marriage and schooling and lower dowry payments. World Bank, *World Development Report on Gender Equality and Development*, 2012, p. 159.

39. United States Global Health Initiative Strategy, 2010, http://www.ghi.gov/resources/strategies/159150.htm.

40. World Health Organization, Department of Making Pregnancy Safer, "Adolescent Pregnancy," *MPS Notes*, vol. 1, no. 1, October 2008, p. 2, based on data provided by National Research Council and Institute of Medicine, 2005.

41. Data provided by the Statistics and Monitoring Section, Division of Policy and Strategy, UNICEF, January 2013.

42. UNFPA, "Marrying Too Young: End Child Marriage," p. 53; Save the Children, "Child Marriage in North Gondar Zone of Amhara Regional State, Ethiopia," 2011, p. 16.

43. Annabel Erulkar et al., *The Experience of Adolescence in Rural Amhara Region Ethiopia* (Addis Ababa: Population Council, 2004).

44. Save the Children, "Child Marriage in North Gondar," citing Pathfinder International, "Report on Causes and Consequences of Early Marriage in Amhara Region," 2006.

45. Equality Now, "Learning from Cases of Girls' Rights," 2012. See also Pathfinder International, "Report on Causes and Consequences of Early Marriage in Amhara Region," p. 35; UN Women, "Five Questions for Muluken Arefaine on addressing child marriage in Ethiopia," October 10, 2012 (estimating that only about half of Ethiopians are aware of the minimum legal age of marriage); UN Women, "Expert Group Meeting: Prevention of violence against women and girls," September 2012, p. 3.

46. Annabel Erulkar et al., "Evaluation of Berhane Hewan: A Program to Delay Marriage in Rural Ethiopia," *International Perspectives on Sexual and Reproductive Health*, vol. 35, no. 1, 2009, pp. 6–14.

47. Population Council, "Evaluation of Berhane Hewan: a Pilot Program to Promote Education & Delay Marriage in Rural Ethiopia," 2007.

48. DFID, "Programme to End Child Marriage: Project Summary," 2011, http://www.projects.dfid.gov.uk/IATI/documents/3707292.

49. Ibid., based on data provided by Macro International, 2008.

50. UNICEF, *Committing to Child Survival: A Promise Renewed*, 2012, p. 23; Anita Raj et al, "The Effect of Maternal Child Marriage on Morbidity and Mortality of Children Under 5 in India: Cross-sectional Study of a National Representative Sample," BMJ, 2010; Nawal M. Nour, "Child Marriage: A Silent Health and Human Rights Issue," *Reviews in Obstetrics & Gynecology*, vol. 2, no. 1, 2009; Santhya et al., "Associations Between Early Marriage and Young Women's Marital and Reproductive Health Outcomes: Evidence from India," *International Perspectives on Sexual and Reproductive Health*, vol. 36, no. 3, 2010.

51. UN, "Goal 5: Improve Maternal Health," *Millennium Development Goals Fact Sheet*, 2010, p. 1, http://www.un.org/millenniumgoals/pdf/MDG_FS_5_EN_new.pdf.

52. Anita Raj, "When the Mother is a Child: The Impact of Child Marriage on the Health and Human Rights of Girls," *Arch Dis Child*, 2010, vol. 95, pp. 931–35.

53. Shelley Clark, "Early Marriage and HIV Risks in Sub-Saharan Africa," *Studies in Family Planning*, vol. 35, no. 3, 2004; Anita Raj, "When the Mother is a Child"; Shelley Clark, Judith Bruce, and Annie Dude, "Protecting Young Women from HIV/AIDS: The Case Against Child and Adolescent Marriage," *International Family Planning Perspectives*, vol. 32, no. 2, 2006.

54. Clark, Bruce, and Dude, "Protecting Young Women from HIV/AIDS."

55. Clark, "Early Marriage and HIV Risks in Sub-Saharan Africa"; Clark, Bruce, and Dude, "Protecting Young Women from HIV/AIDS."

56. Nawal M. Nour, "Child Marriage: A Silent Health and Human Rights Issue," *Reviews in Obstetrics & Gynecology*, vol. 2, no. 1, 2009; Jere Behrman, Harold Alderman, & John Hoddinott, *Hunger and Malnutrition*, 2004.

57. See, for example, Gene Sperling, *What Works in Girls Education: Evidence and Policies from the Developing World*, 2004.

58. Shelley Clark and Rohini Mathur, "Dating, Sex, and Schooling in Urban Kenya," *Studies in Family Planning*, vol. 43, no. 3, 2012.

59. Ming Cong Nguyen and Quentin Wodon, "Child Marriage and Education."

60. G. Psacharaopoulos and H. Patrinos, "Returns to Investment in Education: A Further Update," World Bank Policy Research Working Paper 2881, 2002/4; David Dollar & Roberta Gatti, "Gender Inequality, Income, and Growth: Are Good Times Good for Women?" Policy Research Report on Gender and Development Working Paper No. 1, World Bank, 1999.

61. Murray et al., "Increased Educational Attainment and Its Effect on Child Mortality in 175 Countries Between 1970 and 2009: A Systematic Analysis," the *Lancet*, vol. 376, no. 9745, 2010, pp. 959–74.

62. See, for example, Anita Raj, Research Letters, *Journal of the American Medical Association*, 2012; World Bank, *World Development Report on Gender Equality and Development*, 2012, pp. 158–59. Barbara Mensch et al., "Trends in the Timing of First Marriage Among Men and Women in the Developing World," in Cynthia B. Lloyd et al. (eds.), *The Changing Transitions to Adulthood in Developing Countries: Selected Studies*, 2005, pp. 118–171.

63. International Center for Research on Women, "Too Young to Wed," p. 6.

64. "Forward," *Early Marriage and Poverty: Exploring Links for Policy and Programme Development*, 2003, pp. 11–14, citing Caroline Harper, Rachel Marcus (Save the Children) and Karen Moore, "Enduring Poverty and the Conditions of Childhood: Lifecourse and Intergenerational Poverty Transmissions," *World Development*, vol. 31, no. 3, March 2003; Sajeda Amin, Simeen Mahmud, and Lopita Hug, 2002, "Baseline Survey Report on Rural Adolescents in Bangladesh: Future Directions for Programs and Policy," Kishori Abhijan Department of Women's Affairs, Ministry of Women and Children's Affairs, Government of the People's Republic of Bangladesh.

65. See, for example, MasterCard Worldwide Insights, "Women Owned SMEs in Asia/ Pacific, Middle East, and Africa: An Assessment of the Business Environment," 2010, http://www.masterintelligence.com/upload/251/178/MC84-WomenSME-S.pdf; "Unlocking the Full Potential of Women in the US Economy," McKinsey and Company, http://www.mckinsey.com/client_service/organization/latest_thinking/unlocking_ the_full_potential.aspx.

66. Kevin Daly, "Gender Inequality, Growth and Global Ageing," Global Economics Paper no. 154 (London: Goldman Sachs, April 3, 2007) (finding that reductions in barriers to female participation in the labor force would increase GDP in America by 9 percent, in the eurozone by 13 percent, and in Japan by 16 percent); Sandra Lawson, "Women Hold Up Half the Sky," Global Economics Paper no. 164 (New York: Goldman Sachs, March 4, 2008) (finding that narrowing the gender gap could increase per capita income in several APEC economies by 14 percent, including China, Russia, Indonesia, the Philippines, Vietnam, and Korea.).

67. See World Bank, *Engendering Development*, 2001.

68. D. Tilson and U. Larsen, "Divorce in Ethiopia: The Impact of Early Marriage and Childlessness," *Journal of Biosocial Science*, vol. 32, no. 3, 2000, pp. 355–372.

69. Shelley Clark and Dana Hamplova, "Single Motherhood and Child Mortality in Sub-Saharan Africa: A Life Course Perspective," *Demography* (forthcoming) (finding that between 25 and 50 percent of women in eleven African countries become single

mothers through divorce or widowhood and that in nine of these countries the children of formerly married single mothers are more likely to die).

70. K. G. Santhya et al., "Associations Between Early Marriage and Young Women's Marital and Reproductive Health Outcomes: Evidence from India," *International Perspectives on Sexual and Reproductive Health*, vol. 36, no. 3, 2010.

71. See, for example, Valerie Hudson et al., *Sex and World Peace*, 2012.

72. Beina Xu, "Governance in India: Women's Rights," Council on Foreign Relations, March 5, 2013.

73. Analysis based on data provided by the Statistics and Monitoring Section, Division of Policy and Strategy, UNICEF, January 2013.

74. Ibid.

75. UNICEF, *Child Marriage and the Law*, 2008, p. 23; see also UNICEF, "Early Marriage: Child Spouses," *Innocenti Digest No. 7*, March 2001, p. 2.

76. ICRW, "Child Marriage and Domestic Violence," 2007, pp. 1–2 (citing ICRW, Development Initiative on Supporting Healthy Adolescents (DISHA) Project, 2005. Survey of 998 young married women from Bihar and Jharkhand, India, 2004, reporting domestic violence within the previous six months).

77. UNFPA, "Marrying too Young," p. 47; data provided by the Statistics and Monitoring Section, Division of Policy and Strategy, UNICEF, January 2013.

78. UNICEF, "Early Marriage: Child Spouses," 2001, p. 8 ("the number of prosecutions under the [Child Marriage Restraint Act of 1929, strengthened in 1978] did not exceed 89 in any year between 1994 and 1998").

79. ICRW, "Child Marriage, Laws & Civil Society Action Fact Sheet," 2006, p. 2, http://www.icrw.org/files/images/Child-Marriage-Fact-Sheet-Laws.pdf, citing Department of Health and Family Welfare, Government of Uttar Pradesh, *Population Policy of Uttar Pradesh*, 2000.

80. UNICEF, *Handbook on the Prohibition of Child Marriage Act*, 2006.

81. UNICEF, *Child Marriage and the Law*, p. 27, citing Indian Penal Code § 375.

82. New America Foundation, *Investing in Girls: Opportunities for Innovation in Girl-Centered Cash Transfers*, 2012, pp. 10, 16 (listing conditional payment programs in fourteen states).

83. ICRW, "Evaluating the Power of Conditional Cash Transfers (CCTs) to Delay Marriage in India," 2012.

84. See note 33.

85. World Vision, "Untying the Knot: Exploring Early Marriage in Fragile States," p. 7.

86. Ibid; see also Anita Raj, "When the Mother is a Child"; Human Rights Watch, "This Old Man Can Feed Us, You Will Marry Him," 2013 (on the crisis of child marriage in Sudan); Ruth Eglash and Hani Hazaimeh, "Syrian Crisis Forces Young Women into Early Marriages," *USA Today*, March 7, 2013; Sudarsan Raghavan, "In Niger, Hunger Crisis Raises Fears of More Child Marriages," *Washington Post*, July 9, 2012.

87. "Secretary Clinton Launches New Public and Private Initiatives to Raise the Status of Girls," October 10, 2012, http://www.state.gov/s/gwi/rls/other/2012/198768.htm.

88. USAID, *Ending Child Marriage and Meeting the Needs of Married Children: The USAID Vision for Action*, 2012.

89. United States Strategy to Prevent and Respond to Gender-Based Violence Globally (2012); USAID Youth in Development Policy, 2012; United States Government Action Plan on Children in Adversity, 2012.

90. Violence Against Women Reauthorization Act of 2013, PL 113–4, March 7, 2013, 127 Stat 54; Conor Williams, "Child Marriage Bill Update," *Washington Post*, December 17, 2010 (detailing concerns about reproductive rights that contributed to the failure of child marriage legislation in 2010).

91. G8 Foreign Ministers chair's statement, April 12, 2012, http://www.state.gov/r/pa/prs/ps/2012/04/187815.htm.

92. "On World's First International Day of the Girl Child, UN Calls for End to Child Marriage," October 11, 2012, http://www.un.org/apps/news/story.asp?NewsID=43259.

93. Commission on the Status of Women, "Agreed Conclusions: The elimination and prevention of all forms of violence against women and girls," 57th session, March 4–15, 2013.

94. See The Elders, http://theelders.org/child-marriage/what-are-elders-doing; www.girlsnotbrides.org.

95. Population Reference Bureau, "Female Genital Mutilation/Cutting: Data and Trends," 2008, pp. 2, 5 (listing countries with high prevalence of FGM).

96. World Vision International, "Protecting the Girl Child from Female Genital Mutilation," 2011, p. 8 (explaining the link between FGM and early marriage); J. Richard and P.S.S. Sundar Rao, *The Timing of Marriage* (Vellore, India: Christian Medical College, 1999).

97. UNICEF, "Technical Note: Coordinated Strategy to Abandon Female Genital Mutilation/Cutting in One Generation," 2005, p. 13; see also Gerry Mackie, "Female Genital Cutting: The Beginning of the End," chapter 13, in Bettina Shell-Duncan and Yiva Hernlund, eds., *Female Circumcision in Africa; Culture, Controversy, and Change* (Boulder, CO: Lynne Rienner, 2001), p. 253 (explaining the compounding relationships between social pressure, FGM, and early marriage).

98. The adolescent fertility rate in Senegal is 9.6 percent according to UNICEF statistics, "At a Glance: Senegal," 2010, http://www.unicef.org/infobycountry/senegal_statistics.html. In Senegal, the maternal mortality rate is forty per one hundred thousand live births, the mortality rate of children under five is 7.5 percent, and the infant mortality rate is 5 percent.

99. Equality Now, "Minimum Age of Marriage Update," citing "Senegal: Out of School and into Marriage," *IRIN News*, July 5, 2010; see also Senegal CEDAW Report 1994, p. 5.

100. USAID, "Gender Assessment 2010, USAID/Senegal," 2010, pp. 13, 16, citing field work by Deborah Rubin (Director, Cultural Practice, LLC) and Oumoul Kharyi Niang-Mbodj (*Réseau Africain pour le Dévelopment Intégré*, 2008).

101. See ICRW, "Solutions to End Child Marriage," p. 19; Population Council, "Evaluation of the Long-term Impact of the Tostan Programme on the Abandonment of FGM/C and Early Marriage: Results from a qualitative study in Senegal," 2008, pp. 2, 5; www.tostan.org.

102. Tostan, "427 Communities Abandon FGC and Child/Forced Marriage at Senegal's First Regional Public Declaration," January 22, 2013, available at http://tostan.org/web/module/events/pressID/283/interior.asp.

103. The White House, Office of the Press Secretary, "Coordination of Policies and Programs to Promote Gender Equality and Empower Women and Girls Globally," Presidential Memorandum, January 30, 2013.

104. J. Bruce, S. Chalasani, M. Chau, V. David, and M. Stoner, "Double hot spots: Co-locating investments in adolescent girls to end child marriage and meet adolescent girls' unmet need for family planning" (New York: Population Council, 2012). Policy analysis and research note prepared for London Summit on Family Planning, with support of Nike Foundation, Novo Foundation, and Population Council.

About the Author

Rachel Vogelstein is a fellow in the Women and Foreign Policy program at the Council on Foreign Relations. She is also an adjunct professor of women's human rights at Georgetown University. Prior to joining CFR, Vogelstein was director of policy and senior adviser in the Office of Global Women's Issues within the Office of Secretary of State Hillary Rodham Clinton at the U.S. Department of State, where she served as a member of the White House Council on Women and Girls. An attorney by training, Vogelstein practiced law as senior counsel at the National Women's Law Center in Washington, DC, and was awarded an Equal Justice Works Fellowship to work on women's health policy. She has lectured widely on women's rights, including at the U.S. Congressional Women's Caucus, U.S. Foreign Service Institute, U.S. Department of State, the Center for Strategic and International Studies, and Harvard Law School. A recipient of the Secretary of State's Superior Honor Award, Vogelstein earned a BA magna cum laude from Barnard College, Columbia University, and a JD cum laude from Georgetown Law School, and clerked for the Honorable Thomas L. Ambro on the U.S. Court of Appeals for the Third Circuit.